And Then There Was Light

Stories, Poems, and Devotionals

Vol. 2

SpeakUp Conference

Compiled by
Living Parables of Central Florida

And Then There Was Light

Stories, Poems, and Devotionals

Vol. 2

SpeakUp Conference

Copyright © 2021 Living Parables of Central Florida, Inc.

All rights reserved.

ISBN: 978-1-953114-19-8

Cover Illustration: Dave O'Connell
Cover Design: Bob Ousnamer

Published by EA Books Publishing a division of
Living Parables of Central Florida, Inc. a 501c3
EABooksPublishing.com

Acknowledgements

We'd like to thank the directors of this conference— Carol Kent and Bonnie Emmorey—for encouraging and equipping writers for the glory of the Kingdom of God. We wish to thank Cheri Cowell and her wonderful team at EABooks Publishing for giving us this opportunity. We thank our many friends and family for supporting us in our writing dreams. And most importantly, we want to thank our Lord and Savior Jesus Christ for His gifts—may this book bring You the honor and glory You deserve.

TABLE OF CONTENTS

Acknowledgments — iii

The Introduction — vii

Speak Up Conference

Chow to Chow — 1
Jerry Howard

My Light and My Salvation — 7
Jen Cason

From Darkness Into Light: Intimacy with My Beloved! — 13
Peaches Hall Knaut

Hope In Loss — 21
Kaitlyn Fiedler

Her Transforming Gift of Life — 25
Pam Caylor

Believe — 31
Donita Breeding

An Imperfect Love Story — 33
Nancy J. Smith

That Woman — 37
Nicole Langman

Satan's Lies — 41
Amy K. Collier

IN THE SHADOW OF THE CROSS *Joy Kats*	47
It Was! *Eugenia Curry*	51
Boo Boo Itch *Bethany France*	55
Life After Abortion *Keasha Holloway*	59
A Time to Mourn *Jamie Mason*	65
I Don't Want To Do This, Please Don't Make Me Do This! *Jolene Paquette*	69

The Introduction

When dark turns to light, weakness turns to strength, despair to hope, and death to life—there is a story. The Greatest Story Ever Told begins this way and our stories are a part of this grand story. We invite you to join us for a journey into our darkness and learn how God used those dark places to transform us, our lives, and the lives of those around us. Through poems, prayers, devotions, and stories you will catch a glimpse of the Light that shatters the deepest darkness. Because in the darkest of nights, God is—and then there was light.

Chow to Chow

Jerry Howard

Marine Corps Boot Camp begins benign enough.

The first few days on Parris Island, South Carolina are just administration, ad nauseum. We walked around carrying all that they issued us, and at night coughing up all that we'd smoked before arrival, spitting out from our bodies' reactions to over 50 allergens airborne in the South Carolina oceanic swamp. What we hacked up, we called 'recruit crud."

Our old lives ended on the first Monday, Training Day 1, when our Drill Instructors were unleashed on us. Anyone who thought it was a good idea to join the Marines before this day was immediately convinced otherwise.

A mountain of military paraphernalia appeared before us. 99 different sets of equipment—from uniforms to deodorant, skivvies to band aids—appeared at the center of the squad bay for our oversized platoon. Deafening screams shattered any rare quiet moment; as soon as one Drill Instructor vanished, another appeared, sometimes two. We were forced to observe the torrent of abuse in a locked-body position.

Barely above a whisper, the lead DI commanded, "Recruits, clean up." None of us moved. He shouted, "Drill Instructors, resume training."

Somewhere in the tempest, while under a fresh shower of verbal assaults, I heard someone ask why were weren't cleaning. Suddenly, half of us were immediately ordered to sift through the foothills of gear with no hope of correctly reassigning them properly. Even calling out our nametapes was useless beneath the screeching of our instructors.

After making no progress with moving the mountain, we were introduced to the pit, a moonscape of sand, sand fleas, and the blood, sweat, and tears of every tough guy imposter possessing the lifetime merit badge of Marine.

We were initiated in what we'd come to know as static bear crawls and 8-count body builders. Mountain climbers, one-legged planks, leg lifts, jack knives, and single clap pushups prolonged the anguish. The exercises worked with the grit and filth in the pit to grind off layers of skin and human frailty.

After 10 minutes, drenched and filthy, the platoon ran to the 3rd floor of the barracks. Our instructors shrieked at us to clean them; our nerves were rubbed raw as we understood that failure would result in a return to the pit. Finally, we were lined up and told to strip. Our shower consisted of shuffling under hot and cold spraying streams without soap or hope.

I could still feel grime under my skin when we were told to clothe ourselves—from the mountain. The lead Drill Instructor, "the heavy," picked one recruit to organize us. Somehow, Recruit Stillwater knew what to do.

With an urgency almost impossible to teenagers, we separated everything into piles and began redistributing the labeled items. Not a single word was uttered, an instinctive combat quiet.

Finally ordered to fall in line, we were dressed and ready for chow.

Stillwater handed me a tray, reading my bewilderment. "Chow to chow. Sunday to Sunday. That's how you survive this mess we volunteered for."

I whispered, "What?"

"Chow to chow, Sunday to Sunday, that's how you survive."

"Sure thing, champ." Phony tough could describe us all, me especially. But peace in Stillwater seemed to run deep.

At chow, per regulation, we had 20 minutes to eat. Getting through line took 18, leaving barely time to inhale the food and momentarily sit with the rigidity required by regulation.

Okay, I thought. Chow to chow.

On Sunday, again per regulation, church services were offered. Attendance was not required, but the other option was remaining in the barracks with the Drill Instructors. My old Marine dad used to say there were no atheists in a foxhole, as if it was regulation. Dad never went to church. He complained that churchgoers were hypocrites and money grubbers.

We recruits lined up according to denomination. On my dog tags was stamped "NO REL PREF." Stillwater leaned in: "Chow to chow. Sunday to Sunday."

"Why do you keep saying that?"

"You're going to stay here with the Drill Instructors?"

"No thanks. Not into mumbling and singing lullabies."

"Get in line, stupid."

Stillwater hadn't steered me wrong yet, so I stepped into the Protestant line. DI SSgt Hawkins, alert to even the fart of a housefly, barked. "Recruit Howard just converted!" Eyes locked forward and having not been asked an actual question I didn't take the bait. I stayed quiet, motionless; maybe he'd forget I was there.

Drill Instructor SSgt Hawkins marched us to the Chapel. We were ushered into the sanctuary where we squeezed onto the rows. We were issued the "At Ease" order but remained standing.

Drill Instructor SSgt Hawkins exited through the glass entry doors with purpose. No Drill Instructors were in the entire building. Were they not allowed in? Did they need permission to cross the threshold? Music played softly around us. Had that been on when I walked in?

A speaker approached the lip of the stage, hands raised, finishing a song. His robe was adorned with what I thought to be ancient hieroglyphs.

"Praise God, praise God, please be seated recruits."

I mumbled, "Presenting the lead hypocrite." I returned to poor posture.

After the standard thank you's and hello's, he said, "As a Messianic Jew, Jesus and I share both a rich history of culture and devout love for God."

Someone yelled, "Amen!"

"Jesus came that we might have life and have it more abundantly. He is my Comforter, my Healer, and my Salvation. He makes me lie down in green pastures. He leads me beside still waters. He refreshes my soul."

Another excited recruit called, "That's right!" I rolled my eyes at the stupidity. I saw no comfort in this packed church, no healing for my exhaustion. The only salvation was that I wasn't in the barracks getting yelled at.

But those two recruits who piped up, who agreed—did they know something I didn't? Or were they morons? Morons looked like the best bet.

The preacher went on, "Anyone lying in green pastures lately?"

I chuckled with everyone else. When did I last laugh? Two weeks ago?

Turning to Stillwater, I whispered, "I like this guy."

"It gets better."

The preacher carried on, "Anyone need deliverance from a demon or two? No one? Let me clarify—demons wearing green campaign covers."

The church erupted with laughter. The air loosened.

"Anyone need a comforter? Not for your bed, gentlemen. Your heart."

Yes.

"How about healing? Who has the most bites from sand fleas?" Half the room's arms shot up.

"I know sand fleas. And I know the pit. And the quarterdeck. Before ministry, I was a warfighter, like you. Twenty-five years ago I crossed over from civilian to Marine. Semper Fi, boys!"

The church resounded with, *"Oorah!"*

"You and I, we share a rich history, too. Like Christians, Marines always begin as something else. The difference is that recruits are all equally worthless. But to God, Jesus, and me, you are all equally priceless."

More 'Amens" rose from the crowd, but I sensed they were becoming heartfelt.

"Jesus is here with us today. He's with you in the swamp, in the pit, and on the quarterdeck. He's in your heart, waiting to be acknowledged. That's your part. The acknowledgment. The faith in the unseen. Faith in Jesus allows us to stay calm in calamity, find peace in war. He gives us the ability to move mountains."

Stillwater shouted, "Amen."

Chow to chow. Sunday to Sunday.

The preacher said, "He's calling you now. You may feel Him somewhere in your spirit, your soul, calling. If so, even if you can hear Him only a little, would you come down and pray with me?"

Recruit after recruit went to the stage. I had no urge to pray in front of everyone. I didn't even close my eyes. But I was listening. Perhaps for the first time in my dysfunctional life.

After the prayer was done, the former Marine Messianic Jew with hieroglyphs on his robe burst into a lullaby, *This Little Light of Mine*.

Through my blurring vision, the lyrics were displayed on a projector screen. Regardless, I never sang so loud. There was still a mountain of shame and cynicism for God to move, but that little light of *mine* finally began to shimmer.

Jerry Howard is a Christian, married and a father of four. He is a Marine veteran, writer, speaker and the founding coach at *E4 Leadership & Business Coaching* in Richmond, VA. He is the current President of *The Specialty Companies*, which provides smart solutions in interior design, energy, and construction.

My Light and My Salvation

Jen Cason

Who *"Your word is a lamp to my feet
and a light to my path"*

(Psalm 119:105 ESV).

"… pack your trash and get out!"

I cried alone in a room as messy as my life, my latest attempt at normalcy crumbling like all the others. For most of the previous two decades, I'd followed advice from one self-help guru after another, convinced I could climb up from my difficult past if I found the right "five easy steps." But now, as I stumbled perilously close to the cliff of homelessness, it was clear again I'd been scrambling along the wrong path.

Those who knew my story blamed my dad. When he abandoned our family in the mid-1960s, the news swept like corona virus through our tiny Midwestern town. In school, my older siblings and I endured merciless teasing and scrutiny. Mom refused to discuss it, leaving me to conclude the logical reason for his departure must have been my birth. Clearly, if I were somehow different or better, he'd have stayed, and life would have been normal.

This theme resurfaced in my teen years as an inability to convince anyone I was being touched inappropriately. Years later one of my abusers would be arrested for a 'much more serious act' against another woman, but at that time I was just a 14-year-old from a broken home complaining about a prominent professional in our small community. Over time I got the message: I didn't deserve to be believed or protected there.

In high school, I battled depression by pouring over popular self-help books. I emerged a talented poet, speaker, and debater. A teacher suggested I use my otherwise too-loud voice to read announcements, prayers, and Scripture in our drafty old church on Sunday mornings. I considered it all a stage on which I appeared to be a smart, confident young believer, intent on college and law school; but inside, I distrusted God and disliked myself every bit as much as most of my classmates had.

My good grades in high school earned a prestigious scholarship to a Christian university on the other side of the state. So, without regret I watched that little town fade away in the rearview mirror. On the record, I was a great coed who participated in student government and intercollegiate debate, and I graduated early with high honors. But to the people who knew me best, I must have seemed a paradox of intelligent self-destruction. On the one hand, I did all my homework before engaging in any leisure activity, and rarely missed class without a good excuse. I hung out with the campus Christians, even studying the Bible with them on occasion. But in truth, that had more to do with my interest in one of the guys in that group than my relationship with the Lord.

On the other hand, in my third semester at college, my roommate and I were regulars at a local bar for the Tuesday night beer special, and had no problem leaving the place with about anyone who suggested it. Only God knows how we survived such reckless decisions. The next semester I met the young man whom I believed would change everything. And indeed, he did.

Like my elusive father, he floated in and out of my life for a few years. Post college, his dad orchestrated a job for me in Phoenix, nine hundred miles from home. After only a few months, he was history and the folly of accepting the position was clear, but returning to southwest Kansas seemed just as hopeless.

So, when another young man who barely knew me proposed, it seemed the perfect solution. Looking back, I don't believe I was even capable of loving someone. At the time, however, the fact seemed immaterial to both of us. He thought he was getting a devoted wife and I thought I'd found acceptance, security, and stability. We were both wrong. By the time we agreed to dissolve the mess we called our marriage, we were mentally, emotionally, and financially bankrupt.

And, we had a toddler daughter. She stayed with him because my degree and experience gave me better employment prospects. Even when he decided to move with her to northern California, I didn't fight it—I was convinced she was better off with him and his family than anything I had to offer.

I poured myself into work and other distractions, unwilling to let go of the conviction that I could, should, and would earn the respect I craved. And I continued to make bad decisions. After a man I dated for a few months began stalking me, I moved in with another guy I knew from work. Then I quit my job on a whim to reinvent myself as a consultant.

Months later, there I was, crying in my bedroom. My dark and lonely path away from God had reached its remotest valley. Though above us an ancient evaporative cooler labored loudly against the Arizona desert heat, I could still hear my roommate's recitation of my contemptible life through the door I'd slammed emphatically moments before.

"You're the biggest _____ loser I've ever seen. Pack your trash and get out!"

Sobbing, I dropped to the bed under the weight of spoken fact. As the light from a single, filthy window surrendered to a fog of heavy gloom, my failures marauded through my consciousness like a half-dozen angry rioters obsessed with destroying any remaining hope in my soul.

The rattling cooler became a drum beat of accusations marching through my mind, replaying the abandonment, molestation, isolation, rejection, and depression. Then the tempo quickened, shifting to my many failed attempts at legitimacy through self-reliance.

As the barrage continued, I recognized the self-help psychology I'd trusted for so long was utterly powerless against this legion of darkness about to overrun my soul. Ignorant of the armor of God, I was totally helpless in the fight. I didn't know about the "helmet of salvation," and I certainly didn't have *"the sword of the Spirit, which is the Word of God"* (Ephesians 6:17).

But I did have a loaded revolver. It was right there on the table next to the bed.

As I reached for the gun to permanently end the torment, a soft light appeared. I saw and felt it move, enveloping me like a loving parent comforting his frightened child. I could still sense the chaos around and within me, but through the light, the disorder seemed muted and far away.

Then, somehow, it seeped into my mind. An indescribable peace came over me even as the light confronted the dark and disturbing notions clamoring for attention. Over their accusations, I heard one of the few Bible verses I knew by heart:

*"Yea, though I walk through the valley of the shadow of death,
I will fear no evil: for thou art with me; thy rod
and thy staff they comfort me"*

(Psalm 23:4 KJV).

Before the recitation was over, the charges against me faded to a whisper and then went silent.

I looked down at my hands, folded in my lap. The gun lay unmoved on the nightstand. Still sobbing—but for an entirely different reason—I uttered a clumsy prayer asking God to help me and thanking Him for whatever was coming next.

That day, and every day since, the Lord has given me a future and a hope surpassing anything I could create from even the best worldly advice. Through the awesome power of His Word, I'm able to face any circumstance with the strength of my ever-present Father Defender. Sometimes it appears as lightning to remove static from a dark and stormy sky. Other times it's the gentle warmth of a triumphant sunrise after a long, cold, silent night. Always, though, it's exactly what I need when I need it.

"The LORD is my light and my salvation; whom shall I fear? The LORD is the stronghold of my life; of whom shall I be afraid? ... For my father and my mother have forsaken me, but the LORD will take me in. ... Wait for the LORD; be strong, and let your heart take courage; wait for the LORD!"

(Psalm 27:1, 10, 14 ESV)

Jen Cason is living proof the Bible is no ordinary book. Her quest to know the lifesaving light of God's Word led this learning professional to create *Digging into Scripture Ourselves*, a twenty-question approach to exploring any Bible passage, anywhere, anytime, with anyone or alone. Try it yourself at jencason.com.

From Darkness Into Light: Intimacy with My Beloved!

Peaches Hall Knaut

Once upon a time, in a land so far, far away,

I was that lonely princess, full of pain in the wilderness of the day.

Not knowing what was wrong you see, lost in darkness all the while,

Unknowing I was lost at sea, not knowing how to follow.

So blindfolded, deaf, and dumb, I stumbled in darkness only to hear,

The sound of confusion in my heart, the sound from the enemy of fear.

For you, God, had told my parents, both Adam and Eve to be right,

To not eat of the Tree of Knowledge of Good and Evil, and in their fright,

Mankind you gave a choice of Your Perfect Love so dear,

With the Plan of Your Salvation to save me from the terrors that drew near.

And so, in the suffering of our choices, choices that I could not fully understand,

I gleaned what you had suffered, I learned of the writing in the sand.

For in the trials, I chose to trust you, in the valleys of despair,

And as you drew me close to you, Lord, You bound my heart with Your repair,

For You told me after my wounding, that You promised to restore,

All that the locusts must have eaten, all the devil stole and more.

And as you drew me close to you, Lord, You bound my heart with Your repair.

For you told me after my wounding, that you promised to restore,

All that the locusts have eaten, all the devil stole and more.

For I know that I am One with you and have nothing to despair,

That I am now your precious will, your purpose, and glory all right here.

For my life feels pain like death, as You awaken me in Your Love,

And You've given me a heart of flesh, Your Holy Spirit, like a dove.

For my heart was like a cold dark tomb, imprisoned in my mind;

It was hell to not have known You, confused, bewildered and so blind.

Yes, I have felt such great despair and grief, that bound me with my shame;

For I sold my soul for cheapened love, I sold myself from pain.

Seeing that You appeared to me so briefly, an eternal moment in Your Time,

As You wept for me so lovingly, I did not know that You were mine.

And weeping as I write this, to have thought I caused you pain,

But You wept for me all-knowing, that your pain was for my gain.

You see I did not understand, how Perfect Love casts out all fear,

I did not understand Your Love, in Your Power of Your Tears.

For Your Kindness and Your Greatness, has led me to repent of old;

And Your Presence so gently bathes me, all memories of wrongs foretold.

So, as we danced together, in Oneness, Bride and Groom,

You were snatched away from desperate arms, and to Your Cross of Doom.

A love so shattered with despair, looking upon my wedding dress,

For it was splattered with Your Precious Blood, yet no one noticed my distress.

As I looked up to you, my Beloved, on that cross where You had died,

Your suffering was to save me, Your suffering for Your Bride.

And as I longed for You, my Lover said, "Come to Me, draw close, draw near,"

For you are my Beloved, for you I also long and so call you here.

And so, swept up into Your Arms, on that Cross as we became One,

One in Body, Mind and Spirit, One Beloved, One Soul, One Love.

Being with You I died, so peacefully, now resting on the Cross,

I did feel all your comfort, no more feeling my tragic loss.

For I know that I am One with You and have nothing to despair,

That I am now Your Precious Will, Your Purpose, and Glory all right here.

So, the Church of Christ, My Love, has truly been kind to me,

With tenderness they took us off, the Cross of Calvary.

And then, they lowered me through the roof, paralyzed with thoughts of life,

To the feet of You my Savior, You my Savior, my soul's delight.

So, as I touched Your Garment, with Your Faith in me and me in You,

I knew that I would be forever healed, restored, redeemed, renewed.

When meeting you at the Well, You explained my hunger, thirst, and Life,

That I had been looking for love all over, looking for You in the darkest of nights.

For in seeking You, You Baptize me as the Way, the Truth, and the Life,

Forever loving and leading me with Your Spirit, my Lover, my Son Light.

You have told me that if I seek You, You promise me a great reward,

And now that I have found You, I know I am loved and fully adored!

For I now believe I am Your beloved, and my Beloved is truly mine,

You fulfill my whole heart's longing with Your Love that is so Deeply Divine.

And the Oil of your Spirit that does caress my spirit now,

With Your fullness and such loving grace, in reverence do I humbly bow.

In the distance I hear your still small voice, feeling peace knowing that You are near,

Your Resonance echoes in my soul, a song of Grace and joyful tears.

As You hold me gently in Your Arms, as You lead me to Your Sacred Light,

Your Still Small Voice is in the quiet, in the stillness of the night.

I am now so filled with such gratitude, a gratitude so divine,

For You have healed my broken heart, my Lord, my Jesus, my Adonai.

You have bound me tightly to Your Heart, to caress my soul from storms,

As I feel Your peace and presence, while knowing I am reborn.

Your hands gently touch my face, warming my heart that had gone cold;

As You revive me from a sleep so deep, a sleep of love foretold.

You give it to me freely, even though I had not heard,

That Your Perfect Love comes easy, Perfect Love so undeserved.

For that is why You suffered on a cold, dark night, in pain,

The pain of Your Gethsemane, the pain of Hell disdained.

And all this that I suffered from that cold, dark night, You wept,

For I had been like the Mary Magdalen, judged and sinful was my dread.

Full of guilt for years accruing, listening to the snake like Eve,

But then You told me "Do not listen!" to the lies that I once believed.

For Your Spirit told me to listen to Your Word and Promise True,

Hearing: "There is no guilt or condemnation," for my whole mind is now renewed.

By my seeking You from my shame, You have healed my thinking too,

That to repent from looking at sin, Your Love for me is Truth.

So, as we dance under the lights of heaven, You have waited for me to turn,

For You let me hear You as You speak, there is nothing but Your Word.

You have taught me in Your Timing, that You are my Precious Lord;

My soul refined as You sharpen me, Iron to iron, by Your Perfect Sword.

Trust fulfilled this very moment, the desire of my soul;

Yes, You are Lord of my passionate dance, I am your lover much more bold.

For we have a mission and a journey of original design,

It is about Our Father's House, of Light and Love Divine.

And so, we are Your Family, with Soul Symphonies to gain,

In the Power of Your Merciful Truth, Compassionate Justice, Your Glory Reign.

For my mind, my will, and emotions, have battled when You called me to rest,

With fear and trembling I walk by faith, giving and trusting with all my heart's best.

The Valleys that brought me trials, of which Your Still Small Voice brings joy,

You whisper that You Love me, so get My Harvest, they too need to enjoy.

For now, returning to my 1st Love, there's nothing else I want to do,

Except, be with my Savior, my Beloved, and tell the whole World about You.

So, lead me, my dear Jesus, to your Family to whom You draw me near,

 Asking for our Heavenly Father, to celebrate prodigals we can cheer.

For You are here and Your Love consumes me, with an everlasting fire,

A passion that is never quenched but ignites us and inspires.

And so, we all are Chosen, as we sing in Perfect Harmony,

For Jesus is Our Risen Lord, who resurrected me.

With all the members in the Body, we are the Church now free,

Father, Jesus, Holy Spirit, One God, our loving Trinity.

Do you hear the Lord and Spirit calling, you from up above?

Who suffers waiting just for you, not believing you are loved?

For as we worship in the Spirit, know Our Father loves you more,

Come close because He wants to love you: Believe! You are adored!

After losing a twenty-one-year marriage, Peaches asks, "God, where are you?" Then, seeking Him at seminary, fails morally, dies spiritually, evil binding her soul, stepping into a nightmare she calls Hell. Then, one day, God taps her shoulder, and turning darkness into light, all pain is gone hearing, "Believe!"

Hope in Loss

Kaitlyn Fiedler

In July of 2000, I was eight years old, and my family and I were on our way to the beach. A truck traveling the opposite direction lost control and hit my family's car, tragically taking the lives of four of my siblings and my parents. My older brother and I were the only ones in our family to survive.

I am here to tell you that there is no despair too great for the Lord to conquer. You see, I've experienced loss. Great loss. I know what grief and hopelessness feel like. But I also know what joy and hope feel like in the midst of the pain. As Christians, we don't grieve like those who have no hope. Because of Jesus Christ, we can hold both sorrow and joy simultaneously. We can trust and believe that the sun shines even through the deepest suffering.

My whole world was completely shattered in one instant. My tight-knit family was gone forever. Gone were the chaotic days of homeschool life. Gone were the long afternoons spent playing outside in the creek. Gone were the nightly devotionals my dad would read. My childhood as I knew it came to an abrupt halt. God provided a loving family to raise my brother and I from that point on, however, the years have not been without much hurt and turmoil.

Because of the faith my parents modeled for me at a young age, I had a strong foundation, and I knew that God was there for me. Though everything else was changing around me, I knew that the Lord was unchanging. He became my fortress. He allowed me to wrestle with Him and ask hard questions. In the quiet of the night, when loneliness and fear often crept in, I cried out to the Lord, "Why me, God?... Are you still there?... Do you love me?... Can I trust you?"

Over the years, God's faithfulness proved steadfast. Though I wandered away, He never left my side. He allowed me to question, search, and roam, all the while gently calling me back to Him.

Gradually, instead of "Why?" my question to God became "What now?" It is okay and good to ask God why, but the question is ultimately self-centered. The truth is, I will never understand why God allowed this tragedy to take place in my life. But thankfully, God doesn't call me to understand. He calls me to trust Him. So now, instead of "Why me?" I choose to surrender to God, asking, "What do you want me to do now? How do you want me to serve you with my whole life? And I pray, Lord, help me. Guide me. I need you.

This journey we are on is not supposed to be easy. It's a long, weary, and often painful voyage. John 16:33 tells us, *"Here on earth you will have many trials and sorrows. But take heart, because I have overcome the world"* (NLT). God tells us trials and sorrows will come our way. We should not be surprised when they hit, but instead seek to trust God with how He will use them.

Now, I am married with a new family of my own. It is a great blessing and one that is more than I ever could have hoped for. Growing up, God surrounded me with many friends, family members, and mentors along the way who encouraged me and spurred me on in my faith. Romans 8:28 tells us, *"God causes everything to work together for the good of those who love God and are called according to His purpose for them."* He is working *all things* together for my good and for His glory. In clinging to this truth, I am able to have great hope and joy—even in the pain, in the trials, and in the chaos and confusion of this world.

If you're hurting today, you are not alone. We have no idea all the ways God is at work in our lives—yours and mine! The Lord pours light into all of our sufferings, no matter how dark.

Kaitlyn Fiedler lives near Greenville, SC with her husband and son. She is currently pursuing her MA in Christian Ministries from Gordon Conwell Theological Seminary. She actively volunteers with her church in a grief ministry to help kids process and heal after the loss of a loved one. She brings biblical inspiration to women on her blog: www.abeautifulbelonging.com. You can also find her on Instagram @kaitlyn_fiedler.

Let In the same way, let your light shine before others, that they may see your good deeds and glorify your Father in heaven.

Matthew 5:16, NIV

Her Transforming Gift of Life

Pam Caylor

She sat before me looking so small, so vulnerable, *so afraid*. What had this young girl, well, a woman now, been through? Yes, she was officially a woman now. She was with child. Just 13 years old, she was five months along already. She had taken the bus and was here all alone. I wondered, "Is this how her life is spent, mostly alone?"

As we talked, she was so transparent, so sweetly *"naïve,"* so trusting of *me*. "Lord, help me show her Your love and guide her in Your ways," I prayed in my heart. She had never been introduced to Jesus before, knows nothing of Him, has barely even heard of His Name. It's so shocking to me, that right here *in America*, you can meet a young person who's never had the love of Jesus even offered to her. Yet, *somehow*, God had arranged this divine appointment. This was a moment of destiny: finding out she *is* a Mommy, and simultaneously finding out that the God Who created her also created and destined this baby in her womb (Psalm 139:13-16), regardless of how that came to be. Such darkness this young woman has lived in. I pray I can show her the light of Christ's love, and strike a match that will set aflame a desire in her heart for a relationship with Jesus.

No one knew of her "suspicion" yet. She had not even taken a home pregnancy test. "Okay, here we go," I thought, as I pulled her pregnancy test results from the file. I was already sure of the result: Positive. Yes, she is a woman now. A Mommy. I whispered a quick prayer: "Lord, Your ways are higher than our ways. I don't know 'why' You have chosen this young 'woman' to be a Mommy *now*? But I trust

You, (Ecclesiastes 11:5; 2 Samuel 22:31; Romans 11:33-36). I know that no matter what it "feels" like, or what it "seems" would be "best," *You never* make a "mistake," and You have a wonderful plan for her *and* her baby. Help me break this news to her. Help me comfort, encourage *and* inspire her. Please shine through me, Jesus."

There were lots of tears. We both cried. Her world was rocked to the core. I began to share with Margarita that God loves her so much that He sent His Only Son to die for her, that she is a sinner in *need* of a great, powerful, all sufficient Savior, Whose Name Is Jesus (John 3:16; Romans 3:23-24). She was like a sponge—absorbing every drop of truth and love I could pour out. My heart was singing, shouting really, "Thank You, Jesus, for this divine appointment with this precious young Mommy. Thank You for preparing her heart...*and* mine."

I also shared with Margarita that her baby is just that—a baby—fully developed, just needing more time in her womb to be ready to meet her. We talked about the, oh so obvious fact that she is young. The truth is that she will never be pregnant with her "first" baby again. We talked about the fact that God gives life, He is never confused, and He never makes a mistake. We also talked about all her options: abortion; carry and release for adoption; and carry and parent.

At first, Margarita felt such despair. Yet, her resolve was amazing. She decided that adoption was not an option for her, and she would *not* be getting an abortion. No. Abortion is *not* an option for her baby. She will, *"Choose Life,"* and parent this baby (Deuteronomy 30:19). After all, she already felt her baby move. That's why she sought us out today. She had to know if she was "really" carrying *a baby*. The initial shock and despair had given way to *hope*.

It was time now to send this young Mommy to face the rest of her world, and to tell *her* mom that she is now a "grand mom." She let me pray with her. I gave Margarita her very first "baby gift," a gift bag with a few necessities, a few reminders that she has a real baby in her womb, and a few tokens to help her stay strong in the face of so much confusion sure to come her way. My job (for today) was done. Margarita had received the "Emergency *WOMB Service*" she so desperately needed.

As the next few days and weeks passed, I stayed in touch with Margarita. This was a difficult path. She was pressured to abort her baby. But Margarita had made her choice. No matter what she had to do, her baby would live. Margarita turned 14, and soon, before we knew it, her time to deliver was here. I went to visit Margarita and her newborn baby boy. What a treasure. What an extraordinary gift God had blessed her with (Psalm 127:3). Oh, he was perfect in every way! "Little Davion," I whispered as I gazed into this beautiful, amazing baby boy's face. "What great plans God has for you and your Mommy!"

Margarita never regretted choosing life for her son. In what she thought would be her greatest time of weakness, she found strength she knew nothing of before. But she had gone back into a world where Jesus was never mentioned. Her life took some very dark turns, and she made some poor choices. Yet, through it all, she had Davion. And she had tucked away in her heart the knowledge that Jesus loves her. Somehow, she knew that He was waiting for her, even pursuing her. Little did any of us know just how important this baby boy would be in Margarita's life.

Fast forward about 7 years. Margarita has a fierce love for her little boy Davion. And now, she realizes it is time to deal with some of the things that have haunted her nights, the darkness that only she knows about. There's a church right around the corner from her house, and she decides to take Davion for a "visit." Wow! Margarita never knew what she had been missing. At first, all she could do was cry through the services. Davion loved the church. He decided he needed this Jesus, this Savior. Then little Davion decided he needed to be water baptized, too. This would bring into focus the biggest piece of God's plan for Davion in his mother's life. Ecclesiastes 3:11 tells us that God has, "made everything beautiful in its time, and placed eternity in the heart." Davion's baptism spoke volumes to his mom. Soon after Davion's baptism, Margarita made the final, never turning back, commitment to make Jesus the Lord of her life. She followed her little boy's lead and was baptized on Easter Sunday.

Margarita went on to serve in ministry, helping at youth events, and becoming a youth leader. Then, Margarita made another choice. She returned to that Pregnancy Center where she had first heard of Jesus, where she had learned that she was a mom, to volunteer and try to give back some of the extraordinary love, joy and hope *she* had found there. After a couple of years, she even got a job there. She was able to minister to other moms—some young and afraid like she had been—but now on the other side of a Choice for Life that had blessed her more than she ever could have imagined.

Today, Margarita is still serving in ministry, allowing God to use her journey from the lonely, frightening darkness into the light. She graduated IT school, and Davion is a Sophomore in High School.

Through the dark places, God has truly transformed Margarita as He patiently, persistently pursued her. The darkness has yielded to light. God turned Margarita's mourning into dancing and replaced despair and sadness with hope and His joy, which is her strength. What an extraordinary *'gift of life'* God had given Margarita. Choosing life for Davion motivated Margarita to "choose life" for herself, too! Along with life, she chose to be a better person, a great Mom, surrender to Christ for her family and for her *own* life, and to "break free" of the strongholds that had tried so hard to shackle her. Death has given way to Life: a beautiful, victorious life of service, hope and strength—a bold, brave testimony of a God Who hears, sees, and saves to the uttermost (Psalm 30:11-12; Psalm 34:4-6; Isaiah 40:28-31; Romans 8:28-30; Hebrews 7:25).

Note from the author: If you were pregnant and chose abortion instead of life, and want to heal, there is total forgiveness and peace available to you in Jesus Christ. When Jesus gave His life, He paid for every sin, including abortion. www.Optionline.org can help you find hope near you to begin your healing.

Pam Caylor is a licensed minister gifted in speaking the truth in love and delivering a message of hope, healing, and inspiration. Pam's experience includes motivational speaking, women's ministry leadership, international ministry, post-abortion ministry, and leading the nation's single busiest pro-life pregnancy center for 12 years—with over 36,000 babies' lives saved.

Believe

Donita Breeding

I looked out at dusk just as it began to rain, then came the light,
How I love when the seasons change.
I decided to take a walk around the block to enjoy the atmosphere
Take in all the different smells and the sounds I would hear.
The rain was but a mist now, like a gentle angel's kiss
I heard this saying before, it didn't seem like a myth.
To my surprise, out of the corner of my eye, I spot a deer.
What a magnificent animal; clearly it was as startled as me.
As I took in the aroma lingering in the air, I was at peace—
It was the presence of God that made it possible for me.
Don't turn away when it's obvious to see;
this planet that we live on is so much bigger than you and me.
So spectacular than anyone could ever dream.
First there was night and then there was light, so vivid and alive!
When you take a deep breath, this time just close your eyes - and believe...

"Now faith is the substance of things hoped for, the evidence of things not seen" (Hebrews 11:1, KJV).

"But without faith it is impossible to please him: for he that cometh to God must believe that he is, and that he is a rewarder of them that diligently seek him" (Hebrews 11:6, KJV).

Donita Breeding resides in southwest Ohio, U.S. She enjoys writing short stories and poetry. In 2017 she started a company called, "Servant of God." She has dreams and aspirations to not only write, but speak to others about her unique in counters with God, in hopes of serving God's will.

An Imperfect Love Story

Nancy J. Smith

As he looked across the school gymnasium, a petite girl with long golden brown hair caught his eye. His Science Fair project was on Bridges and hers was on the Human Body. He finally got up the nerve to speak with her and bought her a Coke. A couple years later, they attended their Junior and Senior proms together, but were headed to different states for college.

During those college years there were many hours spent on the dorm hallway phones sharing a Bible study, and almost daily letters mailed back and forth. Summers and holidays they happily reunited, and by their senior year they began planning a blessed future together. He was going to be a civil engineer and she a registered nurse. It was funny how their early interests would become their careers.

Plans for a bright and sunny future suddenly became cloudy, postponed, and uncertain. Her senior year of college she became very ill. Suffering from a rare syndrome caused by a tumor on her right lung, graduation was followed by a trip to the hospital for tests and major surgery. He sat by her bedside praying, while she recovered in the ICU, and he wondered what God was doing. She wrestled with God when they postponed the wedding, because she did not like the change of plans. Yet, God was teaching them to trust Him even through dark days. Her fiancée had proven he would be faithful "in sickness and health." Now, their bond of love and commitment was strengthened, and they chose to thank God for healing and decided to keep Him in the middle of every plan. Their wedding day was a very joyous occasion for all who attended.

After the wedding they started their happily ever after by starting their careers and saving to buy a house. Soon three children came along one right after the other; a girl and two boys. But once again their lives took a different path when the second child was born with cognitive and physical disabilities. That little one came home with tiny casts on his feet and required open heart surgery at six months of age. Their lives now had many real concerns and the future was quite cloudy. Multiple doctor visits and seeing therapists became the new normal. The now mother of three also continued to have her own medical issues. Challenging? Yes. But they knew that nothing is impossible with God.

God never promised a life of sunshine and rainbows. Instead, life is full of good days as well as dark and stormy nights. Trusting in His goodness and sovereignty gave hope that they would find the silver lining. God had been so faithful to them they became involved with a family and marriage ministry to help others. They taught that communication and commitment was essential, while quitting was not an option. The couple also became involved with disability ministries, Special Olympics, and they served together in their local church. This was only possible with God's help and strength.

After 38years the couple still celebrates with gratitude all God has provided. Now in mid-life, they are planning for retirement. The "sandwich years" held their own dark alleys to navigate, but now their parents are gone and the children are grown. The son with disabilities will always need extra help but is doing quite well. Plans can still get rearranged, however, they find security and comfort in each others' arms knowing God is in control. Every day they choose to walk in His light and trust Him in the darker places because love is for a lifetime.

Even when I walk through the darkest valley, I will not be afraid, for you are close beside me. Your rod and your staff protect and comfort me (Psalms 23:4 NLT).

Nancy has a passion for sharing God's word and encouraging others to grow in their faith. Through her blog and speaking ministry *"Securely Anchored"* she brings scripture to life and encourages others to grow in their faith. Nancy is also a retired operating room nurse and lives in Massachusetts.

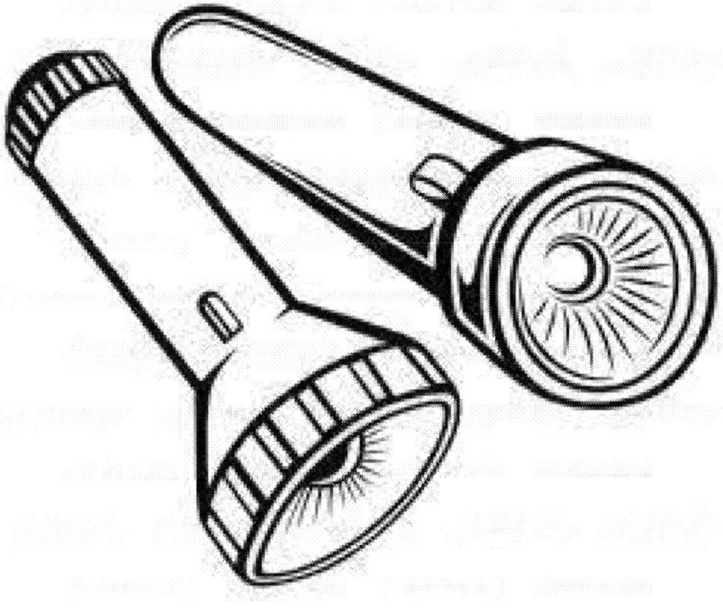

That Woman

Nicole Langman

Her face is beautiful, but shame has called on her to hide behind the many masks that keep her safe—keep her small. Unseen, but fully exposed. Her thoughts are constant and jagged-edged, reciting the vicious chatter she has endured for years.

Undeserving of lasting love. Unworthy of grace. Unclean.

Today, like every day, she waits until the sun is high in the sky before she sets out, knowing that no one will be on the path, safe from the whispers, the sharp words, the judgement. Covered in dirt, calloused from the journey, she hides deeper in her covering as she nears the well.

She bears the scars of brokenness. Rejection. Fear. Around her eyes are heavy circles, telling the world that she is weary—that she has suffered. Her heart bears the wounds of hope denied, time and time again. She does not walk as a woman who knows she is loved, no, this is not her truth. She would crawl if she could.

The dinner parties continue without her. Her absence seems to go unnoticed. The family laughter in the neighbourhood rings loudly in her ears as she longs to provide a home for her children where there is stability, safety, and honour.

What must it be like to raise children with one man, a man they can call Father, a man who stays? She wonders, but she wouldn't know. She is the town harlot, married many times, living with a man she has not married. So many men. So many hurts. So many opinions and suggestions rooted in anything but grace.

To her peers, she is *that* woman. That woman who hasn't learned from her mistakes. That woman who is facing the consequences of her actions. That woman who can't be trusted with the husbands in the group. That woman with the scarlet letter.

Shame follows her to the well on this blistering day, and as she walks, she feels the stares of the many who have fed the hurt and the rejection story that forms her identity.

Outcast. Unfit. Unwanted.

But as with every other day, she pretends. She pretends to not feel it, to not show it, to not give in to the desperate cry of her heart to be understood, to be seen, to be loved.

If only they knew. If only they could see the private road I have travelled, the collection of trauma and wounds that I work so hard to heal. Her heart pleads.

Fear and uncertainty rise up as she notices a man at the well. *A Jewish man.* Her heart beats faster as she wonders about his intentions. Her experiences with men have not been positive. *Jews hate Samaritans; what brings this man here?* She wonders.

The well is a sacred place, a place she feels comforted, a place she can be alone with her thoughts, her tears, her scarlet letter. But today must be different, today she must hold tight to the facade. She moves quickly to the edge of the well, and lowers her bucket.

"Woman, can you please get me a drink?" His voice is deep and gentle.

Heart racing, she is quick on her feet with words. She's had to be, men have asked her for things her whole life. She responds with a coy rebuttal, honed by the many years of turbulence and banter. Mustering confidence she could only hope for, she lifts her bucket from the well, and turns to face this Jewish man who dares to ask her for a drink. *I am not giving this man.....*

Her gaze connects with his.

Everything around her narrows and silences.

And in an instant, there is a knowing—a deep soul knowing, unlike anything she's ever experienced.

My heart! My heart! Messiah?

The pounding of her heart is matched by His.

Love.

There seems to be no one else in the world as she looks at the face of Love, and as everything else fades away, she finds wholeness. Her brokenness meets healing. Her rejection finds redemption.

She feels her scarlet letter fall to the ground, replaced by His words for her, *beloved, beautifully and wonderfully made, wanted, adored.*

This Jewish man knew of her private pain, and her regrets. He gently uncovered hurts she had tried to forget, offered healing for the past, and hope for the future. He reminded her of things in her life that no one could have known, things even she had long forgotten. He told her about the new life He had for her, a new identity, and a new name. She would no longer be *that woman*. Now she was *His*. Chosen and set apart.

Chosen. Set apart. Seen. Adored.

And then, like a whisper, her heart understood. *He was waiting here for me. I am why He was here. This man, The Messiah, waited for me. I am loved!*

She could not contain her joy. Leaving her bucket at the well, she ran back to town, shouting and laughing about what and Who she had just experienced.

Love.

Those who had rejected her, now listened. Her shame replaced by a legacy of redemption and grace. Her sins now forgiven—she was free.

Only Jesus can change pain into purpose and bring beauty from brokenness. Our ancient sister's story, littered with trauma and loss, became a message of hope and healing that would reach through the centuries to touch the lives of thousands.

What would she tell us if she could speak to us directly? Would she remind us of the healing power of Jesus? How a second in His presence heals an entire history of hurt? Would she smile with a knowing smile, having travelled a road like ours, secret sins, painful rejections, disappointments and fears that are hard to say out loud? I think so. And I imagine if we could sit down over coffee with this woman at the well, she would tell us to lock eyes with Jesus, focus on His truth about us, and let Him guide us away from the dark and broken places into His light. We are wanted. We are chosen. And we are free.

Nicole Langman is a therapist in private practice in Ontario, Canada. She considers herself a rejection researcher and writes and speaks to women on the topic of reclaiming their identity in Jesus when life hands out wounds that are hard to heal.

Satan's Lies

Amy K. Collier

I sat on the bathroom floor with my forehead resting on top of my knees. My arms hugged my legs close to my chest. I began to cry uncontrollably as the pain and hurt consumed me. I could no longer pretend to be okay; I am far from okay. The will to fight for a life of peace and happiness beyond the scars that, deep down in my soul, I never believed I deserved, left me.

I whispered to myself, "I know what I have to do; it is the only way. I just can't take it anymore. I am too emotionally exhausted and weak to fight any longer." I slowly stood up, wiped my face, and blew my nose. Taking a deep breath, I opened the bathroom door and walked into the kitchen, focused as if I were on a mission. Unfortunately, it was the same mission I had been on many times over the past twenty-six years.

As I entered the dimly lit kitchen, I quietly searched for the sharpest knife I could find. A sense of accomplishment rushed over me. I found what I was looking for, this is going to save me from the pain I could no longer tolerate.

Sweat ran down my sides and my heart began to pound faster. There was no turning back now. Clutching the knife in my hand I quickly walked back into the bathroom and locked the door. As I walked towards the bathtub, I caught a glimpse of myself in the mirror. With swollen eyes, and tears running down my face, the relentless negative recordings began to play. Just look at yourself. I hate you. You deserve to hurt. You deserve to bleed. You push everybody away.

You can't do anything right. Nobody loves you. You are all alone. You're worthless. Your kids deserve so much better than a broken mother like you.

Sobbing uncontrollably, I sank to the cold, hard floor. As I stared at the knife in my shaking hands, I could hear my heart pound in my ears, my shirt now soaked with sweat, I felt broken. Defeated, I no longer had the strength or will to fight my memories.

You win! You're right. I just want it to stop, it has to stop! I deserve to bleed. I do deserve to hurt.

My eyes remained on the hidden prize clutched so tightly in my hands that my knuckles had turned white. While holding the knife in my left hand I stared at my right wrist, saying out loud, over and over, "I hate you. You deserve this. You deserve to hurt. You deserve to bleed. You deserve all the pain that you feel."

I squeezed the knife tighter in my shaking hand, took a deep breath, and closed my eyes as the blade ran across my wrist. Immediately my wrist started to burn and the blood began to flow. The blade in my hand felt like a part of me; becoming a replacement for the blood that was leaving.

"I hate you. You deserve this. I hate you!!!"

I could not see the extent of the damage through my tear-filled eyes, but deep inside I felt I deserved more physical pain. It was not yet enough. I squeezed the handle again as tight as I possibly could. With every ounce of anger I held deep down inside, I ran the blade across my wrist as hard as I physically could. I yelled out to God, my God, the one who was supposed to protect me, save me, but instead in my mind turned his back on me years ago.

"Where are you? Why won't you protect me from this pain? Why won't you help me? Why do you continue to punish me? Why won't you just let me die?"

I looked down at my wounds; my wrist was covered in blood. It ran down my forearm and dripped into a puddle on the floor. But I could still feel the emotional pain. I could still hear my self-loathing playing over and over, like an audio track on repeat.

A panic rushed over me and I once again drove the filet knife across my wrist, cutting through the already gushing blood. The burning and stinging were stronger, and I took a deep breath.

Suddenly, it all stopped. As fast as the episode started, it ended. I felt like I could breathe again. The tightness in my chest, released. My focus had shifted from the emotional to the physical pain. I felt numb all over, except for the burning of my bloody wrist. It was over. I had made the voices stop.

The next morning, I arrived at my job cleaning houses. I was not aware that Sam had noticed part of the bandage around my wrist sticking out from the bottom of my long sleeve shirt. She asked me to join her and her husband in the living room, and as I sat down on the couch, she asked me if I had tried to hurt myself. Completely caught off guard I burst into tears. She knew I was going through a difficult time. She hugged me and told me that God was with me, and I needed to trust in him. Then she asked if it was all right if she and her husband prayed with me.

She asked God to show His presence to me and comfort me. Before I left, she wrote something on a piece of paper and gave it to me. Inside that piece of paper were written: I can do all things through Christ, which strengthens me.

Two days later I entered a condo at the resort I cleaned for, and I noticed that the sliding glass door leading onto the balcony was open. As I got closer, I heard an elderly woman's voice. "Is anyone there?

"Yes, ma'am it's housekeeping," I yelled.

In a soft, sweet voice she asked, "Can you bring me a bottle of water from the refrigerator and my cane?"

I took a bottle of water from the refrigerator and picked up the cane on my way to the balcony. Sitting outside in a wheelchair sat a short, round, elderly lady with silver hair and glasses. As she looked up at me, her eyes widened and her mouth fell open. I froze at her expression, not sure what to do next.

After a few seconds of silence, which seemed like an eternity, and without taking her eyes off of me, she said, "They are so beautiful. Come closer to me." Tears filled her eyes. I didn't know what to say or do, but for some reason, I felt drawn to her. I slowly walked toward her, gripping her cane and the bottle of water tightly in my now shaky hands.

I set the bottle on a small table beside her wheelchair and leaned the cane up against the table. As I took a step backwards, she leaned forward, still not taking her eyes off me, and grabbed my hand. There was a softness in her eyes, which seemed to see straight through to my soul. I felt like I should be afraid but for some strange reason I wasn't.

She held my hand tight and said, "You are surrounded by angels; you are not alone. I don't know what you are going through, but God brought me here so I could tell you." Chills ran through my body, and I could feel the little hairs standing up on my skin. Immediately tears began to fill my eyes. Don't cry, don't you cry, I kept telling myself.

My fingers squeezed the bottom of my long-sleeve shirt that covered my bandaged wrist. "I have something I want you to have." She pulled out a bookmark from her Bible and began to write along the side of it and handed it to me.

As I read the hand-written words; I can do all things through Christ, which strengthens me, I knew without a doubt that God was trying to get my attention. As I left the condo I looked up to the ceiling and said out loud, "You have my attention, I'm listening."

On my way home I pulled over in a church parking lot and started to cry. "God, why did you abandon me when I was a child? I needed you. I can't do this alone anymore. When I calmed down and became quiet and still, flashbacks from my past began. In a split second, I was seeing clips of the most traumatic events during my life, but unlike my normal flashbacks I wasn't seeing the events that happened,

I was seeing what God stopped from happening. My eyes were opened, God never abandoned me, He saved me from a far worse fate. I am worthy, I am loved. My darkest hour became one of my greatest blessings.

Amy K Collier, has been a guest speaker on radio, pod casts and interviewed for magazines. Amy's life has been a story of hope and survival. She gives hope of living a better life to many others. Amy's most recent work is her memoir, Beyond the Scars.

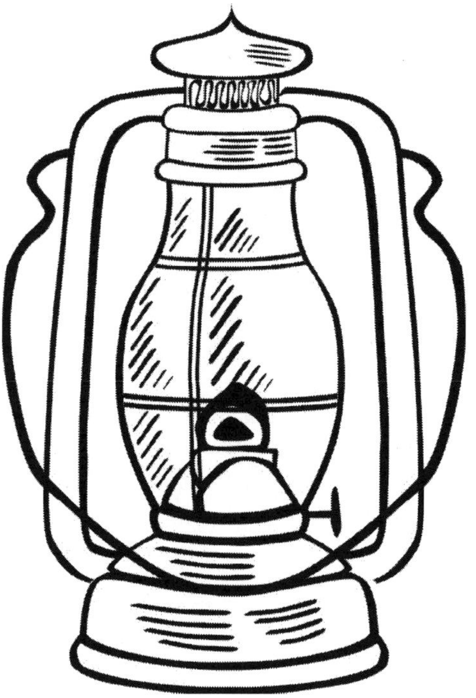

IN THE SHADOW OF THE CROSS

Joy Kats

Step by painful step, I trudge up the rugged hillside. The chains that bind my ankles clink hard and heavy against the stones beneath my feet. I keep my head down in shame and fear, making desperate attempts to deny the fate that awaits me. The weight of my shackles is nothing compared to the burdens that crush my soul. Some days I can barely stand under the pressure of it all.

Sin. Pain. Sorrow. Guilt. In anguish I cry from the depths of my heart.
Oh, how I long for freedom; but none is to be found.
If only there was another way. If only I had another chance.
But it's too late. I'm a dead man walking.

The ground begins to level as I reach the top of the hill. I squint my eyes in the afternoon sun. And there in the shadow stands a wooden cross. I pause for a moment before slowly inching toward it. The reality of my imminent death overcomes me, and I fall to my knees in repentance and regret.

Through my tears I notice fresh blood in the grass. I follow the trail that leads me to the cross, where pieces of flesh still cling and blood stains it red. Knowing that this is soon my death, I turn away. It's simply too much to bear.

But then in the shadow, I see the light. The Light of the World opening my eyes to the truth. This blood on my fingers is the blood of Jesus. Instead of me…because of me…spilled out for me.

O Lord, if you kept record of sin, who could stand?
I now realize this is my death. And yet, I'm still alive. How can this be?

Hear my voice, I call out in earnest. *Be merciful, Lord Jesus; for with you there is forgiveness.* This truth starts to take root in my soul as I sit quietly in the shadow of the cross.

While I wait for the Lord, the burden begins to lessen, and the chains begin to loosen. Still shaky and unsteady on my feet, I slowly stand. I lift my head and shift my gaze toward the now empty cross, even while envisioning Jesus still nailed there. As I run my hand over the splintered wood, I feel the hole left by the stake that held His feet. I hear echoes of taunting and wicked laughter. I smell the unmistakable stench of death. I taste the salt of my own tears as I grapple with the magnitude of what has happened in this place.

My wretchedness for Christ's righteousness.
My sin for His salvation.
My curse for His commendation.
My guilt for His grace.

Here in the shadow, I have hope. For with Christ, there *is* a way. A second chance. For Christ offers steadfast love and overflowing redemption. And with Jesus, there is grace: the merciful kindness of God. This amazing and beautiful gift of unearned favor with the Almighty is offered to me because Jesus endured the horrors of sin and incomparable ugliness of death.

Between the light of heaven and the dark of earth stands the cross. In the shadow it stretches high and deep. And in the shadow, I find all that I need. For in the shadow, I find grace. No more fear. No more guilt. No condemnation now I dread. In the shadow of the cross, I see that His love is longer and wider and higher and deeper than any I've ever known.

In the shadow I see the Light of Life.
For Jesus came to give me life, full and free.
It is for freedom that Christ has set me free!

In this moment, the shackles fall and so do I, once again overcome. Broken. Humbled. Forgiven. This time the weight of sin replaced by the weight of glory. Here in the shadow of the cross, I weep tears of joy and sing songs of praise to my beautiful Savior. I open wide my arms and hold my head high. Jesus loves me, this I know! I step out of the shadow into His marvelous light. The Son, in all His brilliant radiance, shines warmly on my face. I look toward the heavens, and I cannot help but smile. Because of Jesus, I AM FREE!

My chains are gone, and I now run down the hillside. My steps are quick and light as I hurry back to my home, my family, my life. I leave this place eternally changed and forever grateful, transformed from the inside out. I came here a dead man yet leave here more alive than ever before. I can't wait to share this good news. The world needs to know this Jesus; His amazing grace, His glorious freedom, and His matchless gift of eternal life—right now, on this side of heaven. The wonderful truths and light He revealed to me…in the shadow of the cross.

Joy Kats is a writer, speaker, and Bible teacher. She works on a Women's Ministry team and has recently authored her first Bible study, *Free Indeed – Uncovering the Glorious Freedom of Grace*. She and her husband Marc have a married daughter and college-age twin sons. They live in Lowell, Indiana.

It Was!

Eugenia Curry

So dark it felt, it looked

Couldn't be,

It was.

No, no please God,

Not me, not my family,

Not our love, not our marriage,

It was.

Years of joy and toil led to this

We were young, now older,

It was.

I'll cry, I'll plead, I'll run,

Yes me,

It was.

Who, what, why, when,

Did I really miss seeing this?

It was.

A deer, half disabled,

Will she fight and get up to see

what the beauty of the forest

still has to offer

Or choose death, perhaps easier,

It was.

Help me, help me, please

I am wounded

Put everything back together please,

It wasn't.

Confusion, betrayal, disbelief,

brokenness became my friends,

It was.

Support, fellowship, therapy, trials,

His saving grace!

It was.

K Eugenia Curry, M.Ed., M.S. is a newer Christian author. A retired teacher and school counselor, Eugenia lives in central New York with her husband. As parents of two adult children, they recently welcomed a first grandchild, Leila. Eugenia enjoys flower and vegetable gardening, yoga, and Bible-related studies.

In Him was life, and the life was the light of men. The light shines in the darkness, and the darkness did not comprehend it.

John 1:4-5, NKJV

Boo Boo Itch

Bethany France

Kids say the darnedest things. How they pronounce words and arrange phrases can be adorable and we secretly never want them to pronounce them correctly for fear that means they are really growing up. Adults, too, say words and phrases that we believe are correct but are they biblically correct? Are they true, kind and helpful? I realized an opportunity in my words one summer day — maybe you can relate.

Filling the gap between church and naptime can be tricky — I want to wear the toddler out, but not so much so that she falls asleep on the drive home. On this day we had about an hour to fill, so we headed to the park. It was a beautiful sunny day, a light breeze and warm air surrounded us as we moved between various playground activities. My precious 17-month old girl was in a light blue, flowery dress with a matching diaper cover that showed when the breeze ramped up or my girl decided to jump for no apparent reason, other than being joyful. She saw the slide in the distance but her eyes were faster than her feet. Down she went. Even as I stretched out my arms I knew my arms wouldn't catch her because I'm no Inspector Gadget. Tears streamed down her cheeks as her protective brother came running from the other direction. Neither one of us could have prevented the fall and scrape. Such is life; bad things can happen quickly even when we are being cautious and think we are ready for what comes our way. I saw that there was blood so, it was time to go home, get a band-aid and patch up this girl. But while I clutched her head to my shoulder, I instinctively assured, "You're ok! You Are Ok!"

Except she's not—in her little mind. Her world came crashing down when she did. When have you and I repeated to yourselves—"I am not ok. This is not ok. Will I ever be ok?" When you got that call, when you were told the news, when your world became dark and scary, when the rest of the world kept spinning while your world seemed to be stuck, when you felt the sting and pain, did you wonder if you were ever going to be ok? While holding my little girl witnessing her not be ok, even though I knew she would be, I said more comfortingly, "You will be ok. You will be ok."

I'm careful now about these words. Sometimes we are not ok. We are hurt, abandoned, sick, sad, tired, or all of the above. But as Christians, we will be ok. We will be ok. Not right now, maybe; maybe not tomorrow. Maybe longer. But while you might not be ok at this moment and I acknowledge that, you will be ok.

I'm thinking of several friends that are hurting. There is loss, sickness, and unimaginable heartbreak. Are you hurting today? Do you know someone that is? To those hurting, they are not ok right now. It's hard to imagine, for them, when they will be ok. Reassure them with your prayers of comfort and peace, so that they feel loved and know they will be ok. In the meantime, when they don't know if and when they will be ok, use your gift of words and actions to show them love and give them hope. What are you good at? How can you use that gift to help someone going through a hard time? When you reach out to the hurting, it can help them see that with God's love and friends' support, they will be ok. When someone pops into your head, it is not a coincidence. That is God's nudging you to reach out, to be the comfort that someone else needs. Those reach outs can be the sign of hope that a hurting person needs to see. The reach outs and assurances are the light in darkness.

"He comforts us in all our troubles so that we can comfort others" (2 Corinthians 1:4).

Shortly after her cement scuffle, she is ok. Weeks later, she still points to her left knee and says "Boo Boo Itch." (My teaching her to say "boo-boo" or "ouch" resulted in "Boo boo itch" and I really kinda love it.) I silently wonder how much longer she will say "itch" or if she even remembers the actual fall or the pain. Because what I want her to remember most is that she was going to be ok. I want her to remember me, her brother, and her God being ready to console her, as well as other angels God sends to check on us. I say to her, "Baby girl, I will always help you up and tell you that you will be ok ... because you will be."

Bethany France, a widow who writes about hope, grief recovery and being a supportive friend, lives in Michigan with her two children. She believes that God blessed all of us with gifts that can help support others when they need it the most. Her posts are found at Bethanyfranceblog.com.

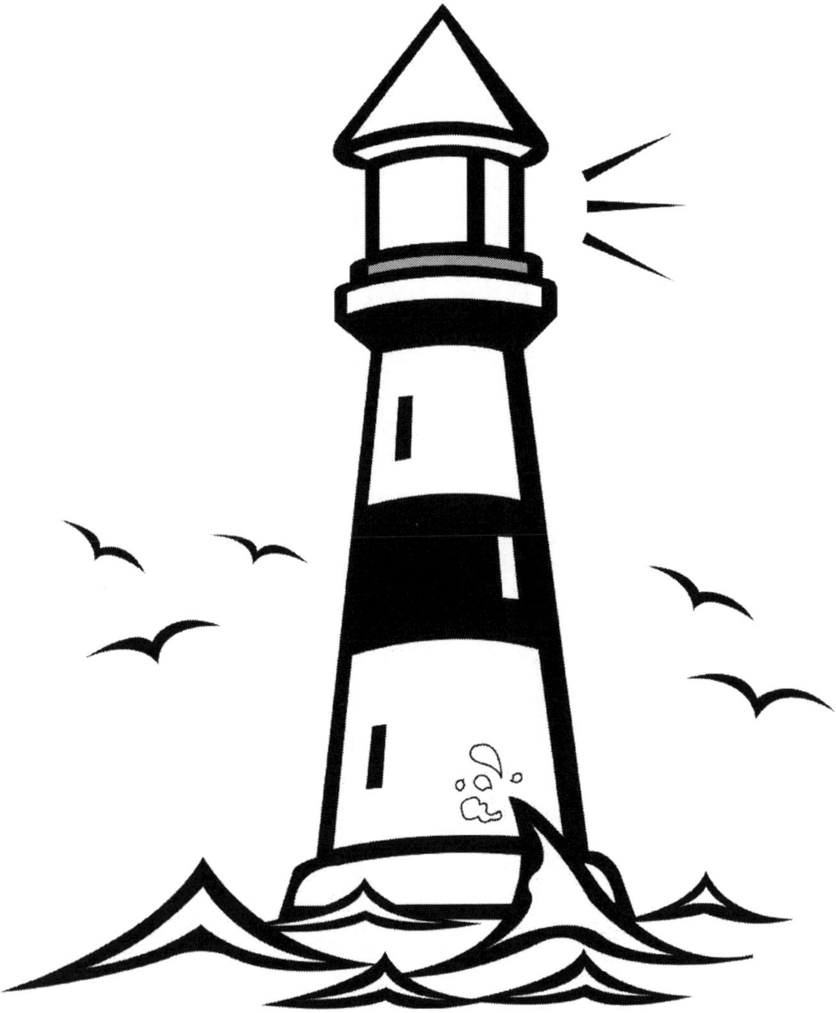

Life After Abortion

Keasha Holloway

The baby girl or baby boy my mama carried before me, aborted.

I guess I'll never know if I had an older sister or brother.

But wait, that could've been me.

Gone, in the blink of an eye. Sucked down a tube, taken from my mama's womb.

Fast forward to 15 years later, now here I sit in a hospital's waiting room.

There are dozens of girls, it's all a blur now, so I really don't remember their faces.

But I do remember the doctor's face and his nurse's, who stood beside him.

Don't move they said, it'll only hurt a little.

Fighting back the tears, as his hand touched my most private part.

My 15-year-old body

Not 1, not 2, but 3 seaweed sticks were what they called them

Packed me up and sent me on my way.

The very next day, in the wee hours of the morning, before the sun showed his face, we were on our way.

The taxi ride there felt as dark as the sky that stood above us.

Now the hospital where we went, was where my mama delivered me.

She pushed me out on a cold November night.

Now I'm back here again, but this time it isn't to give life but to take it.

Just like that, my baby boy or baby girl, aborted.

But wait that's not the end

There would be many more to come. Many more waiting rooms filled with girls. Dozens of girls, some who came with company, but like me most of them came alone.

They promised me I'd be counseled, they said it came along with the package.

A sonogram I never did get to see

Wait, why didn't the doctor ever come to greet me?

They said it was because it was early on, what I carried wasn't a baby at all — they never did let me see.

I'm sure they saw the flicker of their hearts, but they made sure to keep the volume low so I wouldn't be able to hear.

Now here I sit here — my file is at least a few inches thick.

The black and white pictures of all my babies, paper clipped tight.

Out of mind, out of sight.

These facilities promised to give me choices and to help plan my parenthood.

With a simple phone call, they said it could all be taken care of.

They promised that I wouldn't have to think about IT anymore, once it all was through.

Yet, they forgot to mention all of the nightmares I'd have for several years to come.

They didn't tell me that the choices I made would haunt me almost every single day.

Wait — come to think of it, they never spoke of the guilt or shame that having abortions bring.

Or how many times I'd miscarry a child that I so desired to keep.

Till this very day, after 4 beautiful boys, the sight of a pregnant woman still makes my soul weep.

Thankfully through Christ I have come to know the truth.

Forgive me Father, for I was blind, but now I see straight through the lies they tell.

Like the one where they say it isn't a baby at all until it lives outside its mama's womb when, in fact, this is where He formed us all.

Jesus Himself, God in human flesh, formed in His mama's womb.

From the moment of conception, that is when life begins.

Before I had fingers and toes, my very identity was formed in the safety of my mama's womb.

That is where God detailed the prints in my hands.

No one in this world is exactly like me.

These clinics promise us choices, but all they do is peddle lies.

Shedding innocent blood should never be a person's right to decide.

Choosing between the life or death of her very own flesh.

I don't know who these words are for, whether it be for 1, 2 or 3.

It is my prayer that you stop and really think about what your baby means to you.

I pray that these words keep you from making that call.

And to the ladies just like me, I pray for your healing.

I hope you begin to realize that because of His blood, you have been redeemed.

And to the babies I never got to name, I promise that you didn't die in vain.

Mommy will cherish you for all of my days.

Each one of you, etched in my heart.

Now it's time to do my part.

To do whatever it takes to abolish the darkness of Roe V. Wade.

Keasha Holloway is a post abortive woman who found healing through Christ. To find support in your area please visit Silent No More at www.silentnomoreawareness.org

Your word is a lamp to my feet

And a light to my path.

Psalm 119:105, NKJV

A Time to Mourn

Jamie Mason

A year after my stepdad was shot and killed, I felt the call to move to New Mexico with my best friend. We had been friends for over 28 years. She knew me before my walk with Jesus started, and she'd seen a lot of changes in me. Yet, this was the first time I felt God nudge me to move. I had heard about this sort of calling in the past, at a church, I was attending. The pastor and his wife were called to move to another location. That friendship was the closest that I had gotten to a pastor's wife. So, I was disappointed that they were leaving. At the time, my relationship with God wasn't strong at all and I didn't attend church very often. I knew very little about this calling thing and, therefore, didn't understand that "call" to go somewhere else, until now. My mom was sad that I was leaving, but I knew in my heart, I needed to listen to God.

I packed up and moved to the Land of Enchantment. Before I left Kansas I applied for a job at a bank. Then when I got to New Mexico I was ready to go to work. Most of my career was in the hotel business, so this was going to be different. I accepted the job as a bank teller, and it was outside of my comfort zone. I cried almost every night because it was so challenging. I did a good job in the drive-thru that had six lanes. Most of the time I was the only one back there. They said when I got frustrated, I didn't sound like it (I kept it all inside until I got home). On top of that, I was expected to meet my goals of offering credit cards, loans, checking accounts, and all of the other banking possibilities. It was very stressful. Yet, I knew God had me there for a purpose, even if I didn't know what that purpose was.

I went back to Kansas for Thanksgiving and my family came to New Mexico to visit for Christmas. After Christmas, my mom and aunt stayed for another two weeks. It was great to spend that time with my family in my new home.

My friend and I talked a lot about God and how great He is. We often laughed so hard we cried tears of joy and sometimes tears of sadness. She was there to help get me through the tough times. It was definitely a learning experience for me. I went to a church by myself every Sunday I was in town. Soon I started to get close to another pastor and his wife. God is so good. There were days while my friend was at work I would cry without stopping. I continued to ask God why I was in New Mexico. I didn't like to be so far away from my mom and family in Kansas. My son and his family lived 3 hours away, which was a blessing. I would go there on the weekends sometimes, or even just for the day.

My mom got sick the middle of January, so I came home for a couple of days while she was in the hospital. They sent her home with antibiotics and I traveled 12 hours back and forth to New Mexico. Before long, I returned to life as I knew it, and still I wondered why God had me in that place.

One day as I was crying out to God, and I heard Him whisper, "I need you to mourn the loss of Chuck (my stepdad)." Suddenly, I realized I hadn't done that. I hadn't taken the time to mourn for myself. I was trying to keep my family together and make sure everyone else was okay. Then it started to make sense to me. I needed the space and distance to process what happened and to cry for myself.

Not long after, God started opening doors for a job in Kansas. I trusted that God had a plan. I talked to Cody, whom I had worked for before I moved, and he said he would be my boss again. He had become a General Manager of another hotel and said that when I was ready he'd have a position for me. Praise God! I thought my move to New Mexico was going to be a permanent move. However, it only lasted 4 ½ months. In that time God was gracious to show me that I needed to take the time away to grieve the loss of my stepdad and to heal.

Whatever season of life you are in, remember that nothing is surprising to God. He knows it all! When we don't do for ourselves what is needed, He will provide a way for us to get it done even if it's uncomfortable. God provides the time and a space for us to mourn and to heal... and then there was light.

Ecclesiastes 3:1-8:

> *There is a time for everything,*
> *and a season for every activity under the heavens:*
>   *a time to be born and a time to die,*
> *a time to plant and a time to uproot,*
>   *a time to kill and a time to heal,*
> *a time to tear down and a time to build,*
>   *a time to weep and a time to laugh,*
> *a time to mourn and a time to dance,*
>   *a time to scatter stones and a time to gather them,*
> *a time to embrace and a time to refrain from embracing,*
>   *a time to search and a time to give up,*
> *a time to keep and a time to throw away,*
>   *a time to tear and a time to mend,*
> *a time to be silent and a time to speak,*
>   *a time to love and a time to hate,*
> *a time for war and a time for peace.*

Meet Jamie Mason: she enjoys traveling, writing, spending time with kids, grandkids & friends, and most of all spreading the good news of Jesus Christ!

The light shines in the darkness, and the darkness has not overcome it.

John 1:5, NIV

I Don't Want To Do This, Please Don't Make Me Do This!

Jolene Paquette

One child has several missing homework assignments. I have various phone messages and emails pertaining to this matter that I haven't taken time to see. The other child keeps missing school because his stomach hurts, but it doesn't seem to bother his eating or does it? Do I know the answer to this question? Am I even aware how much he's hurting? The lawn needs mowed. Mice are taking over our house. I missed the house payment! Someone has really bad gas…wait did someone poop in my living room? No! The basement has 4-5 feet of flood water with sewer sludge mixed in. HELP! My husband died.

My young, barely teenage, kids have lost their father. I don't want to get up. I can't think. I don't want to think. Let me stay in this chair…please let me stay in this chair. But, I have to get up. What day is it? Is it time for breakfast, lunch, or dinner? Has anyone eaten today? Do I need to cook? I don't want to cook. Is the bus coming? Just let me get lost in my own work. My staff thinks I threatened their jobs if they don't bring me chocolate for my birthday…Oy vey! STOP, the world and let me off. PLEASE let me off!

I can't deal with this. I don't WANT to deal with this. Please, please let me wake up from this dream, this nightmare. I DON'T want to be part of this club…the widow club. Suddenly, all the things that Mike did are crystal clear. Will things please stop getting added to the to do list today, this week, this month, this year. HEEEEEELLLLLLLLPPPPP!

I'm screaming inside. I feel like I'm drowning. Please, let me just float on the abyss of nothingness. Allow me time to not think or feel. NO! I can't feel that right now, lunches need to be made. Dishes need to be done. The funeral home called, they need clothes, and an obituary written by what seems like "yesterday." Pallbearer's wives are calling for details. I hang up. I can't provide details because I must write this obituary in one hour and the phone won't stop ringing! I turn it off.

I grab my laptop, and drive to the cemetery. There I sit in my car and write my husband's obituary. How did we get here? Am I really navigating these cold dark waters? BREATHE! One foot in front of the other, take one step at a time. You can do this — you're strong. You've always been strong. People have always told you you're strong. I DON'T WANT TO BE STRONG! Someone please come and be strong for me. I don't want to be strong. I want to cry. My husband just died last night.

I should cry. I should comfort my kids. Where are my kids? Don't worry, they are not little. They're old enough to take care of themselves. I need to call a Pastor. What's the next step? Food, how many do you expect? I don't know. How do I know? It's a guess, a bad guess. Did I cry for help, yet? Did I scream HELP, yet? Can anyone hear me? Does anyone know what I need? HELP! Please help me, Lord, I can't do this. I don't want to do this. Please don't make me do this. But I have no choice. Your kids are crying, they are taking his body out, call the mortuary, call the Pastor, update Caring Bridge. Did I miss anyone? STOP the train! Let me off. This destination is not on my list, it is not in my plan. My chair, my blanket, the TV droning, useless, but necessary noise, these are the tools I need. Just let me sleep. Why can't I sleep? I'm tired. I've made endless decisions, countless arrangements, answered too many questions, just let me sleep. I don't want to wake up. Who will _____ ? (fill in the blank). How will

_____ ? (fill in the blank) Where's my blanket? The pain, oh the pain, not emotional pain, the actual physical pain. Where are my medications? Someone please take the pain. HELP, pleeeeeeease help! Someone lift me out of this endless darkness. Someone take this heavy weight if just for a day.

Wait, there's the neighbor at 5 am setting up a sump pump to take care of the disgusting stinky, flooded basement. Daylight breaks and others are just showing up to haul away damaged goods. Thank you Lord, there's a glimmer of hope, a miniscule crack shows light through the darkness. Maybe it will be okay. Help is coming.

Kids, we may need to eat peanut butter and jelly or buttered noodles for about 10 days. The phone rings. The Pastor's voice asks if I'm home because he has a delivery. I'm home. Sixty pounds of meat is delivered. Thank You God! The crack is bigger, a few more rays of sunshine glisten through the black, now turning gray, crevices of my mind.

Run away! Work, spend money, travel, go away for real, or in your mind. Do anything to not have to think of reality. Stay busy. You don't have to feel if you stay busy. Where is my blanket and chair? Please let me go back. The light is too painful. What? My kids need me home, but I must work. There's so much to be done. Let me stay away. If I don't see them hurt, I don't have to confront my own hurt. Please turn the light off. Let me wander here a while longer. I don't want to feel.

Rote. Let's do everything as though by remote. Go through the motions, but don't feel, don't think. Finally, sleep, and then aching, body racking sobs. Ugly crying. I'm dreaming of drowning, but instead I'm climbing out of the water. I'm dreaming of Mike holding my hand. I wake up, saying out loud. "I can feel you. I can feel you holding my hand." Thank You God for letting me feel his hand in mine if only for a moment. It was so real. Thank you, Father God.

Who's going to mow the lawn? I am. I may fight rheumatoid arthritis, I may be in pain, but I'm choosing to move, and God provided the tool of an electric start mower from an unexpected source. Who's going to kill the mice? I am, I couldn't set a snap trap, but He showed me a creative way—you don't want to know, but it did the job. Who's going to help kids navigate their feelings and school? I will, and a gracious friend tutored my daughter. The payment got made and fees waived. What are we going to eat, and will I cook ever again after providing convenient food for months? Yes, multiple deliveries of meat were delivered.

Did the stinky floods stop? No, we eventually moved, but each time God broke through and gave me supernatural strength and He kept me safe while plugging in those sump pumps. Was it fun? No. Was it necessary? Yes. Did I grow and learn? Yes.

Each hard thing brought a sense of accomplishment. God empowered me to make decisions, to do tasks I'd never done, and He provided every step of the way. Each breakthrough shed more light into our darkness. Various cracks and crevices are still being illumined.

Do I still have dark moments? Yes. Is God's light prevailing over darkness? Yes. The overarching truth has been that God has held and is holding us through our darkest times, whether lengthy or only a moment. Darkness comes before dawn, but dawn comes. Problems come before solutions, but solutions come. Breaking comes before breakthrough, but breakthrough comes. Darkness lasts for a night, but JOY comes in the morning. We hurt because we loved. God loves us in our hurt and shines His endless light into our darkest places.

If we don't know the valley, we can't appreciate the mountaintop. If we've never been in a dark place, we may not appreciate light. It's a cycle, and everyone's journey is different, yet with similar steps. Light prevails. God shines His light as He leads us, teaches us, and even gently rebukes us, as necessary. Whether breakthrough comes like a burst of sunshine on the brightest summer morning, or seeps through the hazy cracks of a foggy, partly cloudy day, it comes if we let it. If we are watching for it, expectant for it, it comes. Light prevails over darkness.

I can't say there is one hundred percent breakthrough, yet. I have my dark moments. What I can say is God has been there at every turn and is helping me turn toward the light. He is a gentleman. It is now a little easier to celebrate a life that was, than to mourn the death that is. Is it your turn to turn toward the light?

Jolene Paquette is a mom, teacher, widow, speaker, and passionate daughter of the One True King. She just turned 60...WOW!, and is driven to help others who have lost spouses find light in the darkness. Do you or anyone you know need help seeing the glimmer? (jbppower@gmail.com)

Interior Images

Used by Permission

Page 12, Candle, www.clker.com, by Ocal 11-18-07

Page 30, Light Bulb, www.openclipart.org

Page 36, Flashlights, www.clipartstation.com, Maribel Rosa, artist

Page 44, Lantern, www.openclipart.org

Page 58, Lighthouse, www.Cliparts.zone

Living Parables of Central Florida, Inc., of which EABooks Publishing is a division, supports Christian charities providing for the needs of their communities. Ministries are encouraged to join hands and hearts with like-minded charities to better meet unmet needs in their communities. Annually the Board of Directors chooses the recipients of seed money to facilitate the beginning stages of these charitable activities.

Mission Statement
To empower start up, nonprofit organizations financially, spiritually, and with sound business knowledge to participate successfully as a responsible 501(c)3 organization that contributes to the Kingdom work of God.

GPS Grant Program
The goal of the GPS Program: The GPS (God's Positioning System) provides a solid foundation for running a successful non-profit through a year-long coaching process and a grant for start-up needs, eventually allowing these charities to successfully apply for grants and loans from others so they can further meet unmet needs in their communities.

Made in the USA
Columbia, SC
20 September 2021